infuse

Esther

courage in a complicated world

by Diane Averill, Diane Dykgraaf,
Sam Huizenga, and Paul Faber

FAITH
ALIVE®
Christian Resources

Grand Rapids, Michigan

We are grateful for the many comments and helpful suggestions of interested small groups and leaders who contributed to the development of this study through surveys and pilot tests. Special thanks go to Gladys Hunt, a writer of many neighborhood Bible studies, for helpful insights on discussion questions.

Unless otherwise noted, Scripture quotations in this publication are from the Holy Bible, Today's New International Version (TNIV), © 2001, 2005, International Bible Society. All rights reserved worldwide.

Cover photo: iStock photo

Maps: Matthew P. Faber

We welcome your comments. Call us at 1-800-333-8300 or e-mail us at editors@faithaliveresources.org.

ISBN 978-1-59255-356-3

5 4 3 2 1

Contents

Map of Ancient Persia and Media

Map of the Middle East Today

Glossary

Babylon—the capital city of the Babylonian Empire (614-539 B.C.), overtaken by the Medes and Persians in 539 B.C. (see Dan. 6:30-31). Parts of this city are still preserved in modern-day Iraq.

Benjamin—one of the twelve tribes of Israel. When the kingdom of Israel split after the reign of Solomon, the tribe of Benjamin joined with the tribe of Judah under King Rehoboam, Solomon's son. The other ten tribes named Jeroboam as their king (see 1 Kings 12).

citadel—a fortified hill and palace complex, distinguished from the surrounding city

concubine—a secondary wife from a king's extended harem

Esther—Our main character's Hebrew name, *Hadassah,* means "myrtle," and her name *Esther* may derive from the Persian word for "star." Scholars have also suggested that *Esther* derives from the name of the Babylonian goddess Ishtar.

eunuch—a sterilized male, often employed by a ruler as a harem attendant

fasting—an ancient religious practice in which people go without food and/or water for set periods of time (Esther 4:15); in the Jewish tradition this was often accompanied by prayer to God for help in a time of great need (see 2 Chron. 20:2-4). In the regular practice of many religions today, people abstain from food during the day and drink only water; then at sundown they eat certain foods according to tradition in order to maintain their health.

Hadassah—see *Esther*

harem—a group of women in a king's household, including his wives, concubines, and female relatives.

Jehoiachin—the king of Judah who was conquered by Nebuchadnezzar and exiled to Babylon with about ten thousand other Jews in 597 B.C.

Jews—descendants of Abraham (Gen. 12-25) who became God's chosen people by way of God's covenant (see Gen. 17); also called Israelites and Hebrews.

Judah—one of the twelve tribes of Israel. The people of Judah were taken captive and exiled to the area of Babylon in several deportations from 597-586 B.C. Jesus Christ descended from the tribe of Judah (see Matt. 1).

Mordecai—Most scholars agree that Mordecai's name derives from the name of the Babylonian god Marduk. (The Bible mentions several other Jewish people who were given Babylonian names after the conquest by Babylon—see 2 Kings 24:17; Dan. 1:6-7.) Mordecai likely had a Hebrew name, as did Esther (2:7), but his Hebrew name is not mentioned. Mordecai's great-grandfather, Kish, was among the first Jewish exiles to be deported to Babylon with

Jehoiachin, king of Judah. The *TNIV Study Bible* adds this note: "A cuneiform tablet from Borsippa near Babylon mentions a scribe by the name of Mardukaya; he was an accountant or minister at the court of Susa in the early years of Xerxes. Many scholars identify him with Mordecai" (see Esther 2:19; 3:2).

myrrh—a costly plant extract prized for its perfume

Nebuchadnezzar—the king of Babylon (605-562 B.C.) who conquered Judah in 597 B.C. and destroyed Jerusalem ten years later when Zedekiah of Judah, ruling as a vassal king, rebelled in 587. During the intervening years Nebuchadnezzar deported several waves of Jewish captives to different locations in the empire, beginning with King Jehoiachin of Judah in 597. (See 2 Kings 24-25.)

Persia and Media—These ancient kingdoms merged in the mid-sixth century B.C. under Cyrus the Great, invaded Asia Minor (modern-day Turkey), and later overtook Babylon (539 B.C.). By the time Xerxes came to the throne of this kingdom in 486 B.C., it ranged from India in the east to Libya in the west and to the northwest almost as far as Greece.

sackcloth and ashes—Since ancient times, people in the Middle East have worn sackcloth and covered themselves with ash as a sign of mourning and great distress (see Gen. 37:34; 2 Sam. 13:19; 2 Kings 19:1-2).

signet ring—The signet ring given to Haman (Esther 3:10) would have been inscribed with the king's insignia and used for sealing official documents with wax.

Susa—This ancient city dates from as early as 4000 B.C. and still exists today as Shushan in Iran. It is located about 150 miles (241 km) north of the Persian Gulf and is due east of Babylon. The palace complex of Xerxes in Susa has been located and partially excavated. A complication to discovery is that the troops of Saddam Hussein bombarded this site during the Iran-Iraq War (1980-88), leaving many of the architectural remains badly damaged.

talents—A talent was a unit of measure equivalent to about 70 pounds.

Xerxes—Having inherited a large realm, several palaces, and great wealth, Xerxes ruled over the Persian Empire from 486-465 B.C.

How to Use This Study

This Bible study aims to help people engage in lively discussion and learning without having studied the Bible before doing each lesson together.

Maps, Glossary, Timeline

Near the front of this booklet are maps and a glossary that can be useful tools for locating places and the meanings of terms used in the book of Esther. See also a timeline on the next page to find Esther's place and other events in history.

Questions for Discussion

The main questions for discussion are numbered and are in bold print. Along with these questions you'll find points "to think about as you discuss" to help spark ideas for responding to each main question. In addition, you'll often see questions that help us connect the story to everyday life under the subheading "What does this mean to me?"

Please do not feel you have to answer every question in the lesson material. Our goal is to help make Bible study a creative, flexible, exploratory exercise in which you engage with your group and grow to know God and each other better.

Episodes

Some of the lesson materials are divided into Episodes. Together with your group you should feel free to decide whether you want to do all the episodes of a lesson in one meeting, or perhaps do just one or two episodes and then wait till your next meeting to pick up where you left off. The choice is yours!

Follow-up Ideas

At the end of each lesson are ideas that you might like to use for follow-up. These include Explore! activities that can help you learn more about items of interest related to the lesson, develop service projects that help you apply your learning to everyday life, or come up with creative writing or art that connects with the lesson material. There are also movie and video suggestions. Or maybe you'd like to try a recipe for treats often baked to celebrate Jewish Purim festivals (see lesson 4).

Break Away (at-home readings)

After the material for each lesson you'll also find readings for use at home. Take a break with God and do some thinking about the lesson material and how the Lord can use it to shape our lives. If you like, clip these pages out and set them in places around your home or at work where they can remind you to spend time with God. You might also like to memorize some of the Scriptures used in these pieces.

Note: Break Away writers in this study are identified by their initials as follows: DA—Diane Averill; DD—Diane Dykgraaf; SH—Sam Huizenga; PF—Paul Faber.

An Invitation and Prayer of Commitment

If you're searching for a relationship with God, or studying with a friend who is searching, see An Invitation (to believe and commit to God) and a Prayer of Commitment provided at the back of this booklet. These can be helpful in talking one-to-one with God or with someone who is ready to make a faith commitment to God.

Leader's Notes

At the Faith Alive website page featuring this Bible study—at www.FaithAliveResources. org, search for "Esther" and click on the link to "Leader's Notes"—you'll find tips for leading this small group study.

We wish you God's blessing as you participate in Bible study together. Have fun as you learn and grow closer to God and one another!

Timeline

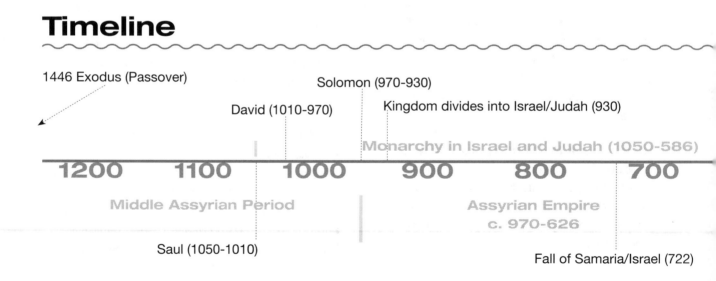

1446 Exodus (Passover)

Solomon (970-930)

David (1010-970)

Kingdom divides into Israel/Judah (930)

Monarchy in Israel and Judah (1050-586)

1200   1100   1000   900   800   700

Middle Assyrian Period

Assyrian Empire c. 970-626

Saul (1050-1010)

Fall of Samaria/Israel (722)

Introduction

In late February the day of celebration arrives. It's the fourteenth day of Adar on the Jewish calendar. Laughter and festive music fill the air. Mouthwatering aromas stir memories of good food and joyful times as people gather and reminisce.

The celebration centers on the story of Esther and her people in the ancient kingdom of Persia around 480 B.C. It's a story of many twists and turns, happy and fearful moments, dangerous and deadly outcomes. It's a story that ultimately points to God's deliverance and care for his people. Scattered throughout the world, watching and waiting for the Lord to act, the Jewish people find joy and hope in the God of their salvation. The Lord's faithful followers trust that

God will keep his promises from long ago, saying he would make their father Abraham into a great nation and bless all the peoples of the earth through him (Gen. 12:2-3).

We know today that those promises point ultimately to the Savior, Jesus Christ. As the Son of God, Jesus brings the greatest deliverance; he suffered and died for our sake so that we can have full life with God forever. Jesus' finished work gives all who believe in him the right to be children of God along with Esther and her people.

As you study the book of Esther, look for the presence and work of God, who watches over and cares for his people always.

Many Jews return to Jerusalem (538-432)

Xerxes' rule in Persia (486-465)

Esther becomes queen (479)

Haman's edict (474)

(Purim celebrated 11 months later)

Birth of Christ (6/5 B.C.)

600 500 400 300 200 100 0 B.C.

Babylonian Empire 625-539

Medo-Persian Empire 539-330

Greek Empire 330-63

Roman Empire 63 B.C. ----->

Prophet Malachi (440-430)

Jewish Exile (586-538)

Fall of Jerusalem/Judah (586)

Prophet Daniel (605-530)

Lesson 1
Living the Life in Ancient Persia

Esther 1

When some people throw parties, they like to do it up big. Break out the fine wines, heap on the choicest foods, and serve it all on designer dinnerware—nothing but the best! Sometimes the occasion is a matter of great joy and celebration. Other times the goal is mainly to impress.

In our first lesson on the book of Esther we meet a king who throws extravagant parties, inviting a multitude of guests to eat and drink as much as they want for weeks and months. And his queen? She's a charmer who turns heads and stops traffic wherever she goes.

Want a closer look? Let's find out more in the Bible's record of these royals dating from around 480 B.C.

Opener (optional)
What might it be like to be married to an extremely wealthy, powerful person? What drawbacks might you have in such a marriage?

Esther 1:1-9
1. What do we learn about King Xerxes in these opening lines?
To think about as you discuss . . .
- the description of Xerxes' kingdom
- Xerxes' banquet, his guests and decorations
- the purpose for all this abundance

Which Esther?
Some Bibles have a different version of the book of Esther than the one in Today's New International Version (TNIV), on which this study is based. That's because some additions and (inaccurate) changes were made in the third to first centuries B.C. in the Greek translation (Septuagint) of the original Hebrew text. The book of Esther in the TNIV is based on the Hebrew manuscript from the fourth century B.C., written before Persia fell to the Greeks in 331 B.C. (see Timeline, pp. 8-9).

What does this mean to me?

- What's your opinion of King Xerxes? How did he run things? Are there people like him in our society today? Explain.

In the days of the Medes and Persians . . .

- **see maps and glossary** at the front of this guide for some background on ancient Persia and Media.
- **see Flashbacks** in each lesson for insights by scholars and history buffs.

FLASHBACK

The ancient Persians were known to put on huge feasts, sometimes with a whole city joining in. The purpose of Xerxes' six-month exhibition and seven-day banquet in 483-482 B.C. may have been partly to celebrate the completion of the Susa palace complex begun by Xerxes' father, Darius. Scholars think Xerxes may have used the event to strengthen alliances and make plans for his military campaign against Greece, launched in 482 B.C. The disastrous battles of Thermopylae and Salamis, both in 480 B.C., were part of that failed campaign.

Because "the citadel of Susa" was the capitol complex, the people described as "the least to the greatest" in Esther 1:5 probably included the king's advisors, officials, and attendants, along with his guests (military leaders, princes, and nobles of the provinces—1:3) and their attendants, but not the common people of the city.

2. What do we learn about Queen Vashti?

Hmmm . . .

- Why do you think she gave a separate banquet for the women guests?

FLASHBACK

Why Vashti gave a separate party for the women is not known, but we do know that the men and women of Persian royalty usually ate together. Some scholars suggest that the women left when the heavy drinking began.

11

Esther 1:10-12

3. How do the king's actions affect the people around him on the last day of the banquet?

To think about as you discuss . . .

- the king's condition and why he might issue such a command
- the queen's response and how this would affect the king

Looking At It Today

This section of the story talks about men's and women's roles in a way that is still often debated today. Let's be careful, though, not to look at ancient Persian culture only through the lenses of our own culture. If you haven't done so already, check out the **Explore!** section of this lesson for ideas on learning more about ancient Persia and other topics of interest.

Esther 1:13-22

4. What does the advisors' suggestion tell us about the culture of that day?

To think about as you discuss . . .

- the reason the advisors give for their suggestion
- whether you've heard reasoning like this in other settings
- the laws of Persia and Media

5. How does the king solve his "little problem"?

To think about as you discuss . . .

- the king's decree and its intended result
- how the decree was delivered

What does this mean to me?

- What do you think of King Xerxes now, and the way he handles things?

- Where do you seek advice? How do you think the Bible could help you evaluate advice that you receive from or give to others?

More to Think About

- How would you comment on this story if you were retelling it to others?

Explore!

Visit your local library or search the Internet for more information on ancient Persia and its customs, Jewish history, and more. A few insightful sources:

- "Women's Lives in Ancient Persia," an essay at www.parstimes.com/women/women_ancient_persia.html.
- See also *Wikipedia: The Free Encyclopedia* at en.wikipedia.org and *History World* at www.historyworld.net.
- Or make your own Web search using combinations of keywords like these: ancient Persia, customs, art, dance, party, queens, kings, Esther, Xerxes, Jews, and more.
- For a fresh translation of an old history of the times, try *Xenophon's Cyrus the Great: The Arts of Leadership and War.* St. Martin's Griffin (paperback, 2007). (Xenophon lived around 430 B.C.)
- Many scholars have shown that the book of Esther is a literary work of art. As you study Esther, look for devices and elements often found in great literature. Read the introduction about this book in the *TNIV Study Bible,* or look for analyses of the book on the Internet. Gather some information, and share it with your group at a later meeting. (See also More to Think About in lesson 4.)

Break Away (at-home readings)

On your own, take some time to relax with the Bible and with God in the coming week. Find a comfortable, quiet place, and have a favorite snack handy. Ask the Lord to help you know him better and to give you insight and understanding through his Word, the Bible, given as our guide to live by. Use some devotional readings like these to help you focus, reflect, and see how God calls us to live. (If you like, use one reading for each of five days, or read a few of them in one sitting. You might also like to clip these out and put them in places at home or at work where they'll remind you to spend time with God.) "Taste and see that the LORD is good" (Ps. 34:8). Enjoy!

Can't Take It with You?

Do not be overawed when others grow rich, when the splendor of their houses increases; for they will take nothing with them when they die . . . .   —Psalm 49:16-17

Xerxes ruled over one of the largest kingdoms in ancient history, and Esther 1 reports that he displayed the vast wealth of his kingdom for more than half a year. Though it's said that money can't buy happiness, a lot of people live as if it does. Psalm 49 expresses some of the limits of wealth. The psalmist notes that we all die, and no one takes their riches with them. Though it's not bad to be wealthy, we are also cautioned: "Do not to be overawed" by wealth or the wealthy. In the New Testament, Jesus reminds us that there's a deceitfulness and even an alluring power in wealth (Matt. 6:24-34; 13:22). Perhaps the deceitfulness gains a foothold when people trust in money rather than God for their security.

Consider how much time we spend each week buying and maintaining things. Is working to make more money harming your relationships, health, or spiritual growth? Are you overawed by wealthy living? Ask God to show you any blind spots you may have about money, and to give you the power to change your actions or attitudes.   —DA

No Restrictions

By the king's command each guest was allowed to drink with no restrictions. . . . —Esther 1:8

What happens when we live with no restrictions? Sometimes we might wish we were free of the rules and other legal things we have to deal with. We might wish there were no speed limits, no taxes, or no restrictions on things that we think are fun and exciting.

But should everyone be free to do as they wish? We might think so—but, sadly, people tend to put themselves ahead of others, and that will lead to hurting someone somehow.

That's what happened at Xerxes' bash. When he was "in high spirits from wine," he thought he would treat his wife as a trophy and as a puppet that he could control as he pleased. That was selfish and foolish, and it created big problems.

Of course, some restrictions can lead to problems too. In some countries people are not allowed to tell others about the God of the Bible, who sent his Son, Jesus, to save us from sin. Other countries have rules that promote racism, and many others turn a blind eye to cultural prejudice based on the color of someone's skin or the ethnic group they come from.

Think about some of the restrictions in your life. Are they set up with good intentions? Are any set up to hurt anyone? Do any need to be changed? Ask for God's wisdom today in all the things you have to deal with and de-cide. (See James 1:5-8.) —PF

Wisdom

The fear of the Lord is the beginning of wisdom; all who follow his precepts have good understanding. —Psalm 111:10

In our Scripture for lesson 1, did you notice that King Xerxes consulted with "wise men who understood the times" (Esther 1:13)? He wanted them to help him decide what to do with Vashti when she refused to be his show-piece. Was their advice true wisdom? Or was it simply the "most reason-able" way to keep from rocking the boat in their culture?

Imagine what might have happened if the king's advisors had "the fear of the LORD" in their hearts and minds. We might have seen a lot more righteousness (justice) "written in the laws of Persia and Media," which could not be repealed (Esther 1:19).

For some insights in the Bible on real wisdom, take a break from your other stuff today and read Proverbs 8. Then just keep going and read Proverbs 9. Then set your sights on Proverbs 1 and include a few more chapters later in the day or maybe tomorrow. "Get wisdom, get understanding" (Prov. 4:5)—it's a free gift God wants us to have!

Here's a little quiz: *Who was the wisest person ever?* Have you ever heard of Solomon described that way? (See 1 Kings 3 and 4:29-34.) King Solomon of Israel was wise—far wiser than anyone around. He wrote thousands of proverbs (see the book of Proverbs in the Bible), and people everywhere marveled at his wise decisions. But later in life Solomon turned away from God, who had given him all his wisdom. Solomon didn't even follow his own advice written in many of his proverbs. Instead, he disobeyed God and "did evil in the eyes of the LORD" (1 Kings 11:6). So Solomon wasn't really the wisest person ever. For the answer to this quiz, see Luke 2:52; Colossians 2:2-3; and Hebrews 4:14-16. Then read Matthew 4-7 and see if it isn't so.

—PF

Furious

"In your anger do not sin": Do not let the sun go down while you are still angry, and do not give the devil a foothold. —Ephesians 4:26-27

Is it bad to be angry? Many people think so, and they have zero tolerance for any expression of anger.

But that doesn't mean all anger is wrong. The no-tolerance idea probably comes from seeing too many examples of badly handled anger. That kind of exposure can set you on edge whenever you see someone get angry.

When Vashti wouldn't let Xerxes have his way, he "became furious" (Esther 1:12). He also nursed his anger and got advice on how to get revenge. That wasn't healthy, and it made problems for a lot of people throughout the empire—all because the king's foolish pride was hurt.

16

So Xerxes' anger was bad. His actions could easily have led someone to think that all anger is wrong. But his wrongdoing began long before he got angry. Xerxes' pride and excess led to drunkenness so that he acted more like a mule than a man (see Ps. 32:9; Prov. 20:1-3; 31:4-5).

Now, when can anger be a good thing? We have to be careful in talking about this, but generally it'll be when we have a good reason for the anger and we handle it in a good way.

For example, it's right to be angry about injustice—such as in the way Vashti was treated. And yet we have to work against injustice in a just way. We may not "give the devil a foothold" in our thoughts, words, or actions aimed at dismantling injustice. That's not easy, but it's the way of God.

Anger and injustice often show up in the same room. How should we deal with these problems? Maybe one way to begin is to see if we have done anything wrong in anger or by showing injustice—and to work on that in our own lives. (See Matthew 7:1-5; Romans 12:9-13:10.)   —PF

True Love

Husbands, love your wives, just as Christ loved the church and gave himself up for her . . . .   —Ephesians 5:25

Xerxes is no model of a good husband by any stretch of the imagination. A capricious despot with a harem cannot be seen as a positive example for husbands. Ephesians 5:21-33, however, gives valuable insight on promoting a healthy relationship between husband and wife. If each person put the other first in their relationship, there would be a lot more contented people in this world.

Jesus is our pattern for loving relationships. He also helps us, through the Holy Spirit, to have the power to live by his example. In addition, he provides forgiveness when we fail, and he gives us the strength to love again— in the way we should.

If you are married, think about ways you can show respect for your spouse, loving him or her as you love yourself. If you are not married, think about friends or family members to whom you can show love "with no strings attached."   —DA

Lesson 2
Search for a Queen

Esther 2:1-18

In this next episode of our story we meet the young woman for whom this book is named: Esther. She soon finds herself caught up in an adventure that many would find exciting and yet anxiety-causing. But this is no Cinderella story. Before long, Esther has to make some important choices.

Opener (optional)
What kinds of things have you tried out for? Did you succeed? Fail? What was it like?

Esther 2:1-11

1. What does the king decide, and how is his decree carried out?
To think about as you discuss . . .
- the events that led up to this decision (see Esther 1)
- the details of the advisors' proposal
- the travel and numbers of people this would involve (see map of ancient Persia near the front of this book)

2. How does this passage describe Esther and her cousin?
To think about as you discuss . . .
- the reason they are living in Susa
- the struggles they probably faced
- see also **Esther** and **Mordecai** and other terms in glossary

What was it like to be taken into exile?

We don't know everyone's experience in exile, but the Bible gives sketches of a few different examples.

- King Manasseh of Judah had led the people to sin against God, "so the LORD brought against them the army . . . of the king of Assyria, who took Manasseh prisoner, put a hook in his nose, bound him with bronze shackles and took him to Babylon" (probably around 650 B.C.). But Manasseh turned back to the Lord, so God "brought him back to Jerusalem" (2 Chron. 33:11, 13; see 2 Kings 21).
- Later (around 605 B.C.) King Nebuchadnezzar of Babylon deported Daniel and many other young men from Jewish royal families and nobility to be trained and put into the king's service (see Dan. 1).
- Esther and Mordecai's great-grandparents were taken to Babylon in a similar deportation (around 597 B.C.) with King Jehoiachin of Judah (Esther 2:5-7; see 2 Kings 24:15-17). Their relatives may have moved eastward to Susa after the Medes and Persians took over Babylonia (around 538 B.C.).
- When Nebuchadnezzar destroyed Jerusalem in about 586 B.C., he "slaughtered the sons of [King] Zedekiah [of Judah] before his eyes and also killed all the nobles of Judah. Then he put out Zedekiah's eyes and bound him with bronze shackles to take him to Babylon." Jeremiah the prophet was at first "bound in chains among all the captives who were being carried into exile to Babylon," but he was freed before the others were deported (see Jer. 39-40).

3. How does the king's decree affect Esther? What happens to her, and how does she respond?

To think about as you discuss . . .

- the way Esther is treated and how much control she has in all this
- why Esther doesn't reveal her nationality
- Mordecai's reactions to this turn of events

Esther 2:12-14

4. Describe the process for each young woman chosen to meet with the king.

To think about as you discuss . . .

- the series of treatments and how long they lasted (see **myrrh** in glossary)
- what a woman might bring along to present herself to the king
- what would happen to her afterward

What does this mean to me?

- What do you think of this process and how people were treated?

- How would this compare with a beauty contest?

Esther 2:15-18

5. How did Esther act when her turn came?

6. What did the king think of Esther, and how did he treat her?

To think about as you discuss . . .

- Esther's manner and what attracted the king to her
- how the king celebrated and the numbers of people involved

FLASHBACK

Esther was first "taken to King Xerxes . . . in the seventh year of his reign" (2:16), so about four years had now passed since Vashti was deposed. This means that Esther became queen in 479/78 B.C. around the same time that Xerxes retired from his failed military campaign against Greece (see Flashback in lesson 1).

What does this mean to me?

- Put yourself in Esther's shoes. How do you think she felt?

- Where do you find strength under pressure?

More to Think About

- Have you ever heard of a story like Esther's before? Do you know of any cultures today in which some of the same things might happen? Explain.

- How much value is placed on physical beauty in our culture? How much is placed on inner beauty? How would you define *inner beauty?*

- We'll get to know more about Esther as we read more of her story in upcoming lessons—but, at this point, what do you think of her? What can you say about her character?

Movie Night?

Sometime toward the end of this study (probably after studying Esther 7), you could have a movie night (with popcorn!) and watch the feature-length film *One Night with the King* (Fox, 2006; 2 hours), based on the Bible's story of Esther. It's available at video stores and libraries or via the Internet. (Take care to follow viewing guidelines prescribed by the production company.) Other movies about Esther are also available. Afterward, spend a half-hour or so on some questions like these:

- How do the movie plot and characters compare to the story you've read in the Bible?

- In what scenes did the script writers have to add to the story to fill in details not mentioned in the Bible? Were those additions helpful? Explain.

- Did the movie change your impression of the story? Do you think that was affirming or helpful? Explain.

Or, for another movie option . . .

Maybe you're up for a historical war action flick on the Battle of Thermopylae, in which Xerxes' troops suffered terrible losses to a small army of Spartans and Greeks in 480 B.C. You could try *Last Stand of the 300* (A&E TV movie, 2007, not rated)—or, for an older cinematic version, *The 300 Spartans* (Twentieth Century Fox, 1962, not rated).

Then discuss a few questions like these:

- What did this movie show that helped you learn something about the time period?

- What mistakes did the invading army make? Are any of these repeated in political maneuverings today? Explain.

- What can we learn from this story in history?

Explore!

If you haven't had the time yet, check out some of the websites and other resources mentioned in the Explore! section of lesson 1. Here are a few more ideas for information on the time period of the Esther story:

- For the Bible's account of the Jewish exile, see 2 Chronicles 36:5-23; Jeremiah 39; and Daniel 1-6. The *TNIV Study Bible* includes helpful notes for understanding these passages.
- At your local library or on the Internet, search for documentary videos on ancient Persia. For example, see *Iran: The Forgotten Glory* directed by Makan Karandish and produced by Mystic Films International (2009). According to the director, "This film . . . is an attempt to recapture the glory of the ancient Persian empires and their influence." (95 min.)
- For a well-written historical novel of the time period, read *Cyrus the Great* by Harold Lamb (Pinnacle Books, 1976).

Break Away (at-home readings)

Take some time again to relax with the Bible and with God over the next several days (or in just one sitting, if you prefer). Remember to ask God for guidance as you begin. Reflect too on your relationship with God. Be assured that God loves you and cares for you. Even in tough times you can depend on God. Though bad things may happen, your eternal soul is secure with him. Jesus promises that no one can snatch you out of his hand (John 10:28), and he says, "I am with you always" (Matt. 28:20).

True Beauty

He has made everything beautiful in its time. He has also set eternity in the human heart; yet no one can fathom what God has done from beginning to end.   —Ecclesiastes 3:11

We've heard the wolf calls; we've seen the leers. Maybe we've even joined in the chorus: "Woo-hoo, what a hunk!" or "Man, what a hottie!"

Queen Vashti was described as being beautiful and "lovely to look at." Esther "had a lovely figure and was beautiful." All the "beautiful young women" taken into the harem at the citadel of Susa "had to complete twelve months of beauty treatments" before spending a night with the king. (See Esther 1:11; 2:3, 7, 12.)

Physical beauty has been prized throughout history and is often seen as a virtue—or at least as a ticket to success.

What does the Bible say about it? Much more than we can fit on this page. Scripture often mentions physical beauty and good looks in descriptions of people, but it does not raise such beauty above personhood, character, wisdom, goodness, or other great blessings that God gives us human creatures. Being able to appreciate beauty is one thing; making it a paradigm or the greatest thing on earth is quite another. And anyone who lusts after beauty strays along the wrong path, away from God (see Prov. 6:20-29)—"like an ox going to the slaughter" (Prov. 7:22).

True beauty, we know, is more than skin deep; it walks hand in hand with real wisdom, following God's ways. While beauty is a wonderful gift, it may not be used in any way to work against our love for God or our love for others (see Matt. 22:37-40).

Make a list of the things you think are beautiful. Are you ever tempted to lust after these things or put them ahead of God and others in your life?

For some additional thoughts, see Proverbs 31:30; Ezekiel 28:12-19; and Philippians 4:8. —PF

Loved, Cared For

To all who did receive him, to those who believed in his name, he gave the right to become children of God. . . . —John 1:12

Our little family includes an adopted daughter. She comes from China. We went there to meet her, sign adoption papers, and bring her home with us to the United States.

What led us to adopt? It was totally "a God thing." I had resisted the idea for quite a while, but my wife brought it up every so often. That was good, because one day I had an unforgettable nudge from God to do something about it. It wasn't a vision, and I didn't hear a voice, but a picture formed in my mind—kind of like the picture of Jesus you see in some children's Bibles and church hallways—and on his lap sat a little girl. She looked like the one in a picture my wife had shown me. And in my heart I sensed the Spirit of Jesus saying, "Will you raise her for me?"

Today, as I write this, she is beaming and celebrating her twelfth birthday. God is good and has taught us many things by adding this dear child to our family. She makes us complete—at least for this generation. She has three big brothers who will always help to look after her. She has a heart for Jesus, and she has often shown wisdom beyond her years. What a precious treasure we have been given!

As I think about Mordecai and Esther, who were cousins, I can see that he treasured and cared for her, his adopted daughter. "Every day he walked back and forth near the courtyard of the harem to find out how Esther was and what was happening to her" (Esther 2:11). In his shoes, I probably would have been racked with grief knowing she'd fallen into the hands of a despot who might do as he pleased with her and throw her away. The only thing left to do was to trust God with her future. This must have been a hard time for Mordecai, and it may have helped him learn things about God that he hadn't imagined.

Did you know that Moses was adopted too? (See Exodus 2:10.) So was Jesus (Matt. 1:20-25). And all who believe in him are adopted into the family of God (John 1:12; Rom. 8:14-17; Eph. 1:3-6). We're loved and cared for, nurtured and cherished, called and taught and purified by the Lord and Father of us all. What's more, as Jesus put it, no one can snatch us out of his hand (John 10:27-30).

Reflect today on some of the amazing ways God has shown his love and care for you. Ask the Spirit of Jesus to help you recognize those things and to help you find ways to tell others about them.   —PF

In His Time

The Lord is not slow in keeping his promise, as some understand slowness. Instead he is patient with you, not wanting anyone to perish, but everyone to come to repentance.   —2 Peter 3:9

How long does it take you to get ready to go out? I have three daughters. When they were growing up, one of my daughters could get ready in ten minutes; one took twenty minutes; and one took nearly two hours. Good grief! It often seemed that all my energy went into training her to speed up that process.

We live in a hurry-up society. It seems that faster is better. When my computer takes a few minutes to boot up, I get impatient. We want instant or quick results.

But some things take time. Raising children takes time. Developing lasting friendships takes time. Becoming a person of great character and beauty takes time. We see that Esther submitted to one year of preparations for her appearance before the king. We too are preparing for an appearance with the king of the universe. And I, for one, am glad that God is patient and has given me a lifetime to prepare.

Today's challenge: pause for a few minutes to reflect on the beauty of your life. What needs more time and attention? What needs less time?   —DD

Everyone Is Welcome

Let no eunuch complain, "I am only a dry tree." For this is what the LORD says: "To the eunuchs who keep my Sabbaths, who choose what pleases me and hold fast to my covenant—to them I will give within my temple and its walls a memorial and a name better than sons and daughters; I will give them an everlasting name that will endure forever."

—Isaiah 56:3-5

In Esther 1-2 we read about eunuchs who served the king. Eunuchs were castrated males. Often they were slaves who had been taken captive or poor villagers who were pressed into the king's service (see 2 Kings 20:16-18). Their lack of sexual desire and their inability to reproduce made them good candidates to supervise the king's harem—a large group of attractive women.

Because of their deformity, eunuchs who believed in God were not allowed to worship with God's people (Deut. 23:1). A prophecy in Isaiah 56:3-5, however, gives a beautiful picture of how God includes all kinds of people who come to him in faith and trust. And a New Testament story about an Ethiopian eunuch who comes to believe in Jesus wonderfully fulfills the prophecy in Isaiah (see Acts 8:26-39).

We need to ask ourselves, How grateful am I of God's acceptance? How careful am I to accept people who are different or for some reason are not fully accepted by others? Are there any ways I can be more welcoming of people from other cultures or backgrounds?

—DA

Favor, Approval

She won his favor and approval more than any of the other virgins.

—Esther 2:17

Does it seem that the king chose Esther on the basis of good looks alone? That's not really likely. The king may have been a prideful despot, but some of the things he did showed that he wasn't stupid. In fact, some of the other women may have been better looking than Esther—at least to some observers. As we sometimes say, "beauty is in the eye of the beholder."

What then brings favor and approval? Why would the king choose Esther? After reflecting a bit, we might think it had to be Esther's talents, poise, charm, wit, smarts, and other qualities that often make people more attractive or desirable than others, even if those others happen to be "lovely to look at" (Esther 1:11). Esther may have had some or all of those qualities that could lend to having a fine, appreciable character.

But could there also have been more? Because we know this book is part of the Bible and it tells an important part of the story of God's people, we might also see that God had something to do with the king's choice of Esther as queen.

When we think about God's working in our lives, we realize we are not the ones in control. Though we can make plans and decisions and do right or wrong things, we can't control things that happen to us—such as aging or accidents. We often can't even control our own tongues or our thoughts. But we may also know that "in all things God works for the good of those who love him, who have been called according to his purpose" (Rom. 8:28).

If we believe in God, we know that ultimately we receive God's favor and approval through Jesus, who came to save us from the curse of sin and death (John 3:16; 5:24; 8:31-36). Because we are called to serve God's purposes (which are always good but are not always easy to figure out), we know we are loved, whether we find ourselves in good times or bad (John 10:27-30). Esther faced both, as we will see later in her story.

How can we show that we appreciate God's favor, no matter what happens? How can we tell others about it?   —PF

Lesson 3
"For Such a Time as This?"

Esther 2:19-4:17

Esther, a young Jewish woman, has become the queen of King Xerxes, ruler of the vast Persian Empire around 480 B.C.

What happens next? Does Esther just sit around looking beautiful the rest of her life? In our Scriptures for this lesson, we learn of conspiracies, anger, racial hatred, manipulation, danger, loyalty, self-sacrifice—and Esther finds herself in the midst of it all.

In other words, the plot thickens.

Opener (optional)
Describe your favorite way to deal with sibling rivalry (either yours or your children's).

EPISODE 1

Note: This lesson material is divided into episodes. Together with your group you should feel free to decide whether you want to do all the episodes in one meeting, or perhaps do just one or two episodes and then wait till your next meeting to pick up where you left off.

Esther 2:19-23
1. What did Mordecai find out "at the king's gate"?
To think about as you discuss . . .
- why Mordecai might be "sitting at the king's gate." (See **Mordecai** in glossary.)

FLASHBACK

The *TNIV Study Bible* notes that "the gate of an ancient city was its major commercial and legal center. Markets were held at the gate; the court sat there to transact its business."

2. What happened after Mordecai informed the king?

To think about as you discuss . . .

- how Mordecai got word to the king
- what became of the conspirators

The background illustration is an engraving of a palace of Xerxes.

3. How would you describe Mordecai's relationship with Esther?

To think about as you discuss . . .

- how Mordecai kept contact with Esther (see also 2:11)
- how you picture them communicating
- how Mordecai had raised Esther (2:7, 20) and the person she had become

What does this mean to me?

- Why is it important to have a connection with a relative or other mentor in your life? If you have a relationship like that, describe its impact on you.

EPISODE 2

Esther 3:1-6

4. How did trouble develop between Haman and Mordecai?

To think about as you discuss . . .

- what the king did for Haman
- Mordecai's actions and the fact that he was a Jew
- why Haman might react so strongly

What does this mean to me?

- How do you respond when your conscience and the law collide?

- How do you deal with people when power goes to their head?

FLASHBACK

The description of Haman as an "Agagite" may give us a clue about Mordecai's refusal to bow to him. Scholars say this may identify Haman as a descendant of Agag, a king of the Amalekite people. The Amalekites and Israel (the Jews) had long been bitter enemies (see Ex. 17:8-16; Deut. 25:17-19; 1 Sam. 15). If Haman was an Amalekite, that could explain his deep hatred not just for Mordecai but for all of the Jews.

Esther 3:7-15

5. How did Haman devise a plan for revenge?

To think about as you discuss . . .

- Haman's explanation to the king, in which he doesn't identify the people who "are different"
- Haman's tactics, and why the king would let him do as he pleased
- how the orders were made official, copied, and distributed

These photographs show a gold signet ring and an impression of the seal of Xerxes.

FLASHBACK

- The date and the *pur* (lot) mentioned in Esther 3:7 are significant. This episode happened "in the twelfth year of King Xerxes," which means Esther was in her fifth year as queen; and scholars note an irony in that Haman begins plotting against the Jews in the month of Nisan (known as Abib in Hebrew), the same month in which the Jews celebrated Passover to highlight their release from slavery in Egypt (Ex. 12). In addition, notes the *TNIV Study Bible,* "the celebration known as Purim [in memory of the story of Esther] takes its name from the plural" of *pur* (see Esther 9:26).
- Haman's offer of "ten thousand talents of silver" would weigh about 700,000 pounds. Today that would amount to about $165 million (U.S.).
- The king's signet ring, given to Haman, represented a transfer of royal authority. This ring was inscribed with the king's insignia and used for sealing official documents.

EPISODE 3

Esther 4:1-5

6. How did the edict (decree) affect Mordecai and other Jews throughout the provinces?

To think about as you discuss . . .

- what Mordecai and others did in response
- what Esther learned about Mordecai
- the fact that Esther didn't know about the decree

Esther 4:6-8

7. How did Esther learn about the edict, and how could she possibly help?

To think about as you discuss . . .

- what Esther and Mordecai had to do to communicate
- the fact that Esther had a secret identity (2:10, 20)
- how bewildering all this would be for Esther

Esther 4:9-17

8. What would Esther risk by bringing this matter to the king? Why?

To think about as you discuss . . .

- the purpose of the law about approaching the king
- that the king had not called for Esther in thirty days
- the minimal power and influence Esther had, although she was queen

What does this mean to me?

- Has keeping a secret or maintaining a loyalty with someone ever put you in a dilemma? If so, how did you decide what to do?

9. How does Mordecai's reasoning show his trust in God?

To think about as you discuss . . .

- the insight Mordecai has, and where it comes from
- the reasoning he uses to make his point

10. What does Esther's decision tell us about her, and how does she involve her people (the Jews)?

To think about as you discuss . . .

- the purpose and practice of fasting in the Jewish community
- what Esther is willing to give up for her people

Check out the glossary for an explanation of **fasting**.

What does this mean to me?

- Have you had to make a decision that could cost you dearly? What options did you have?

"three days" (Esther 4:16)—In the Jewish culture the number 3 often served as a symbol of holiness and completeness (see Isa. 6:3; Rev. 4:8). See also Jesus' comments in Matthew 12:39-40. Note also how the number 3 is perceived in conventional wisdom: a tripod or a three-legged stool is remarkably stable; a third party is often helpful in settling disputes. "A cord of three strands is not quickly broken" (Eccles. 4:12).

Explore!

If you haven't had time to search for more info about the life and times of ancient Persia, look back to the Explore! sections of lessons 1 and 2 and see what may interest you there. Here are a few more ideas:

- Coin collectors: Maybe you're intrigued by ancient forms of money and commerce: talents, shekels, scales, marketplaces, and more. To get started, try http://ancienthistory.about.com/od/coins/Coins_and_Money_Ancient_Coinage.htm.

- Actors, dramatists, stage designers, directors: Maybe you're beginning to picture a drama you could put on for your church or community, based on the story of Esther. Try googling the following and see what you get: Esther, plays, costume, design, stage, ancient Persia. One helpful site might be www.jewish-theatre.com.

- At your library or on the Internet, check out some of the works of Herodotus, a Greek historian from around the time of Esther. For a free e-book by Herodotus, visit www.gutenberg.org/etext/2707.

Break Away (at-home readings)

Can You Keep a Secret?

"A city on a hill cannot be hidden. Neither do people light a lamp and put it under a bowl."   —Matthew 5:14

When you tell someone a secret that you've promised to keep, it's not much of a secret anymore, is it?

Esther kept her family background a secret. Have you wondered why Mordecai would tell her to do that? We learn later that Mordecai himself did not keep his background a secret (Esther 3:4). But perhaps he thought it would be safer for Esther if the king and others in the palace didn't know she was a Jew.

Esther was really good at keeping her secret. We also learn later that she revealed it at just the right time to help her people. But that's a part of the story that comes later.

In the New Testament we learn that God revealed an important secret at just the right time too. Galatians 4:4-5 tells us, "When the set time had fully come, God sent his Son, born of a woman, born under law, to redeem those under the law, that we might receive adoption to sonship." This means that God sent Jesus to save us from sin so that we could become children of God and live forever with him. (Actually God had been hinting about Jesus' coming for many centuries; he just hadn't said when it would happen.)

And now that God's secret is out, it's good news for all people (see Luke 2:10). So there's no need to keep it a secret—let's share the good news of full life with God, made possible through Jesus!

How can you share the good news of Jesus with others today?   —PF

A Festering Sore

He himself is our peace . . . and has destroyed the barrier, the dividing wall of hostility. . . . His purpose was to create in himself one new humanity . . . to reconcile them to God through the cross, by which he put to death their hostility.   —Ephesians 2:14-16

Much of the story in the book of Esther revolves sadly around people's hatred for one another. Haman has a deep-seated hatred for the Jews. Apparently he is a descendant of the Amalekites, an ancient nation that fought bitterly with Israel, the ancestral nation of the Jews. The feud between Haman's people and Mordecai's people went back more than a thousand years (see Ex. 17:8-16; 1 Sam. 14:47-48). And apparently it still simmered just beneath the surface of social politeness, ready to heat up anytime.

The story of racism in our world is no less sad today. Almost every conflict in nations around the globe today goes back to ethnic feuding and grudges that have been nursed for centuries, if not thousands of years.

Jesus came to break down the dividing walls between nations and peoples, offering everyone new life as "fellow citizens with God's people and also members of his household" (Eph. 2:19).

Jesus gave up his life to bring all people and God back together again. Do we have to change anything in our lives to show we want that too? Pray for healing from the sin of racism in this world, and ask God to help you see how you can be a part of that healing. —PF

Money Talks

Keep your lives free from the love of money and be content with what you have, because God has said, "Never will I leave you; never will I forsake you." —Hebrews 13:5

The Bible has many good things to say about money. Wealth and prosperity are blessings from God, and they can be helpful for building up the kingdom of God. But if we fall prey to money's allure and we lust after it to build up a kingdom for ourselves, we find no real happiness or contentment— only sorrow, stress, loneliness, and eventual destruction.

Haman had lots of money. Some historians say his offer of 10,000 talents of silver was two-thirds the amount of the yearly income of all Persia. Whether or not that was true, Haman knew the power of money and how it affected people, so he used it to throw his weight around.

Did you notice how Haman used money to bully King Xerxes? Haman wanted so badly to kill the Jews that he offered the king a ridiculous sum as a bargaining price to get his own way. Haman was basically saying, "I want this edict, and I have the power to become a major shareholder in your kingdom, so let me have it!"

Now let's consider what might have happened if Xerxes had agreed to take the money: he could have become Haman's puppet for the rest of his life. But that didn't happen. Xerxes, perhaps wisely, said, "Keep the money"— but then he gave Haman what he wanted anyway.

See how money talks? All it took was the *threat* of being controlled by Haman's money, and Xerxes found himself backed into a corner. With people plotting against his life all the time (see Esther 2:21-23), Xerxes knew he needed powerful allies and protectors. And since Haman with his vast wealth was so powerful, Xerxes didn't want Haman as his enemy. So the king handed over his signet ring and told Haman to do as he pleased (Esther 3:10-11).

One of the beautiful lessons in the Esther story is that even though Haman and his money were powerful, they were no match for the power and mysterious workings of the God who protects his people.

Who would you rather have watching your back? Ask God today to protect and bless you, knowing that you depend totally on him. —PF

Unlucky 13th?

"The God who made the world and everything in it is the Lord of heaven and earth. . . . From one man he made all the nations . . . and he marked out their appointed times in history and the boundaries of their lands." —Acts 17:24-26

Some scholars suggest that Haman summoned the royal secretaries to write his edict on the 13th day of the month because the number 13 was considered unlucky. We can't be sure if that's why Haman did that, or if maybe the secretaries had just run out of ink and had to wait till the 13th to receive their next supply. But if the choice of the 13th day had anything to do with superstition, would that really have made a difference?

Others have thought the choice of this day was strategic because the 14th day of the same month was for the celebration of the Jewish Passover. This yearly feast celebrated the people's deliverance from slavery in Egypt (see Ex. 12). But if Haman really wanted to "get their goat," couldn't he have had the edict written *on the same day* as the Passover? All we know for sure is that the Bible doesn't say why the edict was written on the 13th.

As for luck and superstition, God will have none of that. When his people lost sight of true worship and just went through the motions by attending feasts and observing holidays ("holy days") without regard for God, he stormed at them, "Stop bringing meaningless offerings! Your incense is detestable to me. New Moons, Sabbaths, and convocations—I cannot bear your evil assemblies" (Isa. 1:13). Instead, said the Lord, "Learn to do right! Seek justice, encourage the oppressed. Defend the cause of the fatherless, plead the case of the widow" (Isa. 1:17).

God wants our hearts and our compassion. God wants true religion with backbone, not some wishy-washy bunk based on superstition. The Lord who knows the end of our days and numbers the hairs of our heads calls us to serve and trust him faithfully. That's all that really matters in our lives.

What can we do to serve God faithfully today?   —PF

Bewildered

Come and see what the Lord has done . . . . "Be still, and know that I am God; I will be exalted among the nations. . . ."   —Psalm 46:8-10

Haman and his power tactics had sent everyone's minds spinning. "The city of Susa was bewildered" (Esther 3:15). And "in every province to which the edict and order of the king came, there was great mourning among the Jews, with fasting, weeping and wailing" (4:3).

When Esther learned what had happened, she didn't know what to do. She knew Mordecai was right; she had to try to plead for the king's mercy somehow. But how? And when? And what could she possibly say or do to change a law in this land where the king's decrees could not be repealed? And what if her approach to the king got her killed?

Somehow, Esther's thinking cleared, and she knew what she had to do. She would fast, and this meant she would not only cut back on carbs and proteins but also pray to God for insight and for the courage to rely on God's strength to deliver his people.

Do you think God himself may have helped Esther see what she had to do? Has God helped you in a way like that before? What happened in that situation?   —PF

Lesson 4
Behind the Scenes

Esther 5-6

God carved out for himself a people, the Jews, promising that all other peoples would be blessed through them (Gen. 12:3). But they often walked away from God and brought trouble on themselves. Still God was merciful and worked in and through the people's lives, often behind the scenes, keeping his promises. Sometimes it seemed that God was silent, but God was always there, watching and working to help his people, even though they might not notice.

Some of the Jewish people, like Mordecai and Esther, remained faithful to God. They remembered stories from their parents and teachers about God's deliverance from slavery in Egypt (Ex. 3-12), the crossing of the Red Sea (Ex. 14-15), and the rule of judges and kings and queens who served God and the people, bringing blessing on their nation as well as other nations. And even though they were now scattered in exile (Esther 2:5-7), God's faithful people waited to hear and see the Lord act again in history.

Let's discover what's happening in and behind the scenes of the fast-moving drama of today's lesson. To save her people from being wiped out, Esther has been preparing to risk her life by approaching the Persian king. What will happen to her?

Opener (optional)
Describe the last dinner or social event that you planned. What made it good (or not)?

EPISODE 1

Note: This lesson material is again divided into episodes. Together with your group, feel free to choose whether you want to do all the episodes in one meeting, or perhaps do just one or two episodes and then wait till your next meeting to pick up where you left off.

Think of today's session as a play with several scene changes.

Scene 1—Esther Acts

The scene has been set for today's lesson. Haman has manipulated King Xerxes into signing the edict to kill the Jews. Mordecai has informed Queen Esther. Now Esther acts.

Esther 5:1-8

1. Chapter 5 begins on the third day of fasting requested by Queen Esther (see 4:16). What action does Esther take?

To think about as you discuss . . .
- the preparation taken by the Jewish community
- the risk for Esther

What does this mean to me?
- How do you think you would have felt in Esther's place?

2. How does the king respond to Esther's presence in his court?

To think about as you discuss . . .
- the king's initial reaction
- the generous offer to Queen Esther

What a Relief!
Archeologists have discovered a relief (wall sculpture) that depicts a Persian king on the throne with his golden scepter; the image may be of Darius (Xerxes' father) or Xerxes himself.

What does this mean to me?
- How would you respond if you were told you could have virtually anything you wanted?

3. How might Esther's request prepare the way for helping her people?

To think about as you discuss . . .
- the invitation and who is invited
- the role hospitality could play in Esther's favor
- the king's repeated generosity
- Esther's second invitation, with an added promise

FLASHBACK

King Xerxes' phrase **"even up to half the kingdom"** was an idiom of the day, not to be taken literally (see also 5:6; 7:2). In their *Commentary on the Old Testament* C. F. Keil and F. Delitzsch explain that this is "a short expression for: if [your] request relates even to the half of the kingdom, it shall be granted." See Mark 6:23 for another example.

4. Why do you think Esther asked for another banquet? (It can be interesting to explore this speculative question if you have time. But there is no right or wrong answer.)

Here's a take on the second banquet, from the *New Interpreter's Bible Commentary* (Vol. 3, Nashville: Abingdon Press, 1999; p. 908):

"[Esther's] request seems anticlimactic, but in reality it is part of a clever stratagem. In [this] society, one never makes one's major request right away. Rather, through a series of minor requests that are granted, the road is paved for the major request. . . . By getting Ahasuerus [Xerxes] to accept her hospitality, Esther obligates him to her and makes it more likely that he will grant her next, larger request. The inclusion of Haman is likewise strategic: She will have her enemy in her own territory and under obligation to her, rather than as a free agent in the court. The king, by granting her request, thereby obligates himself to her and realizes that he is doing so."

What do you think of this interpretation?

Scene 2—Haman Reacts

A scene change occurs in the drama: Esther has invited the king and Haman to another banquet, and there's a growing tension in the air. The following scene portrays the next six hours or so in Haman's world.

Esther 5:9-14

5. List the words in verse 9 that describe Haman's emotions. What does this section show us about Haman's character?

To think about as you discuss . . .

- the change in emotions as Haman exits the palace and heads home
- Haman's description about recent events, and his wife and friends' response

What does this mean to me?

- Are there ways to celebrate our success without bragging? Explain.

- How does our anger sometimes get in the way of making good choices?

EPISODE 2

Scene 3—The King's Discovery and Haman's Surprise

Meanwhile, back at the palace . . .

Esther 6:1-3

6. How does the king find out about Mordecai's loyalty? How could this help Mordecai?

To think about as you discuss . . .

- the account that is read to the king (see Esther 2:21-23)
- the timing of this discovery
- the king's response

Esther 6:4-10

7. How do Haman's plans for Mordecai suddenly change?

To think about as you discuss . . .

- Haman's intentions for coming to see the king at this time
- the king's question and Haman's response to it
- Haman's motives and desires

Journaling? Chronicling?

Have you ever tried journaling as a way to track important events in your life? Journaling can be a meaningful exercise for anyone who likes to reflect. It can also help you remember things that have happened to you over the years. And you don't have to do it every day—once a week, once a month, or even just occasionally will do.

Looking back can be a fun exercise, stirring warm and humorous memories. It can also be insightful and thought-provoking. Many people have found that going through their old journal has helped them see God's activity in their lives—sometimes God intervenes in clear, dramatic ways, but most often God works quietly behind the scenes, guiding us, protecting us, as we see often in the story of Esther. If you've journaled in the past, maybe you'd like to share an example or two that speaks of God's behind-the-scenes care in your life.

8. What great irony happens here?

> **irony:** incongruity, often humorous, between what a person expects and what actually happens

Scene 4—Haman Honors Mordecai

This scene takes place in public—throughout the city—and then closes quickly back in Haman's domain.

Esther 6:11-14

9. What would this turn of events mean for Haman now?

To think about as you discuss . . .

- the picture of Haman bringing the royal robe to Mordecai and leading him around the city
- how Haman feels as he does all this, and afterward
- Mordecai's thoughts and emotions during this event

10. What do you think of the prediction made by Haman's wife and friends? What impression does this give you about their beliefs?

11. Do you see God working behind the scenes in chapter 6? Explain.

More to Think About

- When or where have you seen the work of God in your life?

- Are there situations in our nation and around the world today in which God is working behind the scenes? Explain.

- Has anything happened lately in your life that has caused you to wonder, "Was that a coincidence, or could that have been God helping me?" Explain.

- Scholars have noticed many dramatic and literary devices in the story of Esther (suspense, irony, parallelism, foreshadowing, flashback, plot twist, back story, symbolism, the cliffhanger, and the "ticking clock" [threat of impending disaster]). Describe ways that this story can help give you insight into the drama of your own life.

- How can you share with others what you've learned from this episode in the Bible?

Have you noticed that **the book of Esther doesn't mention the name of God?** Why is it even in the Bible? Rabbi Irving Greenberg, a Jewish scholar, says that in the people's acceptance of the book of Esther, they "showed their grasp of the way to understand how God acts in history in the post-prophetic age. They realized that God [usually] operated not as the force crashing into history from outside but in the center of life as the One who is present in the "natural" and in the redemptive process," in which God works in and through people. —from *The Jewish Way: Living the Holidays;* see www.myjewishlearning.com/holidays/Purim

Explore!

- Do you like to write? How about plotting out the story of your life on a timeline? Draw some icons to add interest, such as a spotlight to highlight major events, and a spyglass (small telescope) to pinpoint specific times when you know God has been working behind the scenes. You could write chapters of your story based on chronological age (for example, Chapter 1: Birth to 10 years; Chapter 2: Ages 11 to 20; and so on). Or you could write sections based on the spotlights you drew on your timeline, and you could weave your spyglass events throughout those sections. Be creative and have some fun! Reflect on God's working in your life story and how you might share that with others.

- For a fun read-through of the story of Esther, read the entire book in one sitting from *The Message: The Bible in Contemporary Language,* a paraphrase by Eugene Peterson. You can find it at your local Christian bookstore or access it free online at www.biblegateway.com.

Eat!

Here's a traditional favorite food that Jewish communities use to celebrate the story of Esther. Though they have a funny name, these pastries are delicious! For a fun treat, plan ahead to share these goodies during your final lesson of this study. Enjoy!

Hamantaschen (Haman's Pockets)

Ingredients for dough

1 cup (240 ml) sugar

1/3 cup (80 ml) margarine

1/2 cup (120 ml) orange juice

3 tsp (15 ml) baking powder

1 egg, beaten, for glaze

1/3 cup (80 ml) oil

3 eggs

4 cups (950 ml) flour

1 tsp (5 ml) salt

For filling

Use apricot or prune jam. Or if you can get a can of poppyseed filling, you can make the traditional poppy seed hamantaschen. For untraditional variations, try other types of jam, chocolate spread, or chocolate chips.

Blend sugar, oil, and shortening. Add eggs and juice. Add dry ingredients and roll into a ball. Refrigerate for one hour. Divide dough into four parts. Roll out each piece very thin (1/8 inch; 1/2 cm) on a floured board. With the rim of a glass or a cookie cutter, cut circles into the dough.

Place 1/2 to 2/3 teaspoon (2-3 ml) of filling in the middle of each circle.

To make into triangles
Pull together the right and left sides of each circle so that they meet in the center, leaving the bottom side down. Lift the bottom side up to meet other two sides, forming a triangle. Seal the sides very lightly; they will ease open in the oven, revealing the filling.

Preheat oven to 350 degrees Fahrenheit (180°C). Brush dough with beaten egg before baking. Place on greased cookie sheets. Bake for approximately 20 minutes. Yields 4 dozen.

—adapted from http://purim.spike-jamie.com/recipes2.html

Q. Why do Jews eat hamantaschen pastries during Purim?
A. The tradition to eat hamantaschen at Purim began in Europe. The word *hamantaschen* derives from the name of a German pastry called mohntaschen, which comes from *mohn* (poppy seed) and *taschen* (pockets), meaning "poppy seed pockets." *Hamantaschen* means "Haman's pockets," referring to Haman's pockets filled with bribe money.

The most popular explanation of why Jews eat this three-cornered pastry on Purim is that Haman wore a three-cornered hat. Eating an image of Haman's hat is a way to symbolically destroy his memory.

Another explanation for the Purim hamantaschen tradition comes from the Midrash (Jewish commentaries on the Hebrew Scriptures). The Midrash describes Haman bent over, covered with shame, and humiliated (literally with clipped ears). The three-cornered hamantaschen are symbolic of Haman's clipped ears. In Hebrew, hamantaschen are called *Oznay Haman* ("Haman's ears").

Yet another explanation for the popularity of the three-cornered pastry on Purim is cited in *The Jewish Book of Why* by Alfred J. Kolatch. He writes that Esther derived her strength from her ancestors, and the three corners of the hamantaschen pastry represent the three patriarchs (Abraham, Isaac, and Jacob).

—adapted from http://kosherfood.about.com/od/purimfoodfaq/f/
why_hamantashen.htm, © 2009 by Giora Shimoni. Used with
permission of About, Inc., at www.about.com. All rights reserved.

Break Away (at-home readings)

Use the following readings to spend some time with God again. How's the relationship going?

Desert Time

O God, you are my God, earnestly I seek you; my soul thirsts for you, my body longs for you, in a dry and weary land where there is no water. —Psalm 63:1 (NIV)

All Christians spend time in the desert. Not the literal desert with sand, sun, and scorching heat. But a "desert place" of total dependence and need. There are times in our lives when we are stripped of all of our capabilities and simply cry, "God help me!"

The Bible tells the story of Joseph, once a favorite son who found himself in an Egyptian prison (Gen. 39:20). Daniel was obedient, and yet stood face to face with hungry lions (Dan. 6). Young Mary woke up one morning still a virgin, but pregnant (Luke 1). Esther and her God-fearing community of displaced Jews were served a death sentence (Esther 3).

The desert place is not somewhere we *choose* to go. It's often something that happens to us and is "not fair." The only choice we have is how to respond. We can choose to trust in the God who loves us more deeply than we can imagine, or we can choose anger and bitterness.

Reflect on your life. Whatever place or circumstance you find yourself in, ask God for the grace and strength to stand as Esther did. —DD

Let's Eat!

On this mountain the LORD Almighty will prepare a feast of rich food for all peoples, a banquet of aged wine—the best of meats and the finest of wines. —Isaiah 25:6

Feasting is a major theme of the book of Esther. Have you noticed how many times a banquet is given? Ten banquets are recorded in this short book. There was a lot of feasting going on!

We also have a culture of eating and banqueting. Think of the holiday celebrations or birthday dinners we have when family or friends gather around to enjoy food, desserts, and each other. These times are a gift of face-to-face relational time. We come together equally in need of food for the sustenance of life and friendship for the fulfillment of love. The lawyer and manual laborer, the four-year-old and the eighty-year-old, single or married, male or female, able-bodied or impaired—all belong at the table.

In these seemingly ordinary events we experience life at its core. Children and parents share thoughts, and close friends share their hearts.

Why wait for the next holiday to celebrate? Make the next meal you share a celebration of life and love, thanking God for sending both!   —DD

Good Story

The earth is the Lord's, and everything in it, the world,
and all who live in it. . . .   —Psalm 24:1

"Read it again!" I barely had the last sentence read, and I heard these words from my three-year-old daughter. It was Cathy's favorite book, and nothing pleased her more than to turn back to the beginning for another adventure with *Harry the Dirty Dog*.

We love a good story, don't we? Think of your favorite book or movie. Stories have a way of involving our thoughts and emotions that transports us to another realm, yet connects us with reality at the same time.

Eugene Peterson writes this about the Bible: "The Scriptures, simply by virtue of their narrative (story) form, draw us into a reality in which we find ourselves in touch with the very stuff of our humanity; what we sense in our bones *counts*. It is a story large with the sense of God, a world suffused with God, a world permeated with God's spoken and unspoken word, his unseen and perceived presence, in such a way that we know it is the world we were made for, the world in which we most truly belong. It isn't long before we find ourselves imaginatively entering the story, taking our place in the plot, and following Jesus" (from *Eat this Book*, Grand Rapids, Mich.: Eerdmans, 2006).

Esther's is a compelling story. Yours is too. Learn to look for God's "unseen and perceived presence." Ask God to show you a world permeated with his presence.   —DD

How's Your Serve?

"The Son of Man did not come to be served, but to serve, and to give his life as a ransom for many."   —Matthew 20:28

I love to serve dinner to my family. Nothing pleases me more than when they all come over and enjoy the food I've prepared. There are other times, though, when I'd rather be served. It's a privilege to have others prepare food and take care of other details for you.

But it's not always easy to work behind the scenes without recognition or honor.

Esther is the center of attention in her own story, and Mordecai is mainly a servant. He is the cousin who takes her in and raises her when her parents die. He cares enough to stay close when she moves to the king's harem. He thwarts a plan to assassinate the king and remains in the background. He encourages Esther to be all that God has called her to be, making her the heroine of the Jewish race. Mordecai is a servant leader.

I respect leaders who serve, who aren't afraid to get in the trenches and work. I admire those who lead with love, always having the best interests of others in mind.

Jesus is the prime example of that kind of leader. When he was on earth, he walked *with* his disciples. He healed, fed, wept for, and loved people. He submitted himself to a Roman cross for the benefit of the human race. He was the ultimate servant.

Esther and Mordecai put their hope in God, and the Lord saved them. Jesus came to show us how to love and live in service to others.

Are there any ways you might improve your serve?   —DD

Chosen

You are a chosen people, a royal priesthood. . . .   —1 Peter 2:9

You've been chosen . . . to receive a coveted scholarship, to be on the team, to take on a special job, to be loved, and so on. It's an amazing feeling, isn't it? Your close friends chose you. Your spouse chose you. Your employer chose you. God chose you. Just as Esther was chosen to be royalty, so were you!

In 1 Peter 2:9 we read, "You are a chosen people, a royal priesthood, a holy nation, God's special possession, that you may declare the praises of him who called you out of darkness into his wonderful light."

Do you feel chosen? Do you act like royalty? I wonder how Esther felt the day she became queen. I would guess that even in her humility she held her head high. Wearing royal robes must make one feel special. When Mordecai was chosen to be honored by the king, he must have felt special too.

In God's large plan of salvation we don't have to be Jewish to be God's chosen people. We are adopted into his family through Jesus. He gives us the right to be called the children of God (John 1:12). That makes us relatives of Queen Esther, Mordecai, King David, and ultimately Jesus—royalty indeed!

Enjoy what it means to be God's chosen royal possession today.   —DD

A Great Eucatastrophe

Esther 7-8

J.R.R. Tolkien, who wrote *The Lord of the Rings*, coined the word *eucatastrophe*, meaning "good catastrophe." This unusual word describes a surprise happy ending that occurs in a story when all seems lost and there's a sudden turn of events for the better. Tolkien taught that all good fairy tales and other stories have eucatastrophe.

Today's lesson from Esther 7-8 covers one of the great and true eucatastrophes of the Bible. When all seems lost, a complete reversal of fortunes follows.

Opener (optional)

Do you like movies with a happy ending? Why or why not?

EPISODE 1

Esther 7:1-6

1. How did Esther present her request to Xerxes? What did she reveal?

To think about as you discuss . . .

- the way she presented herself
- her emotions as she made her request

2. How did Esther's news affect Xerxes and Haman? Compare and contrast their reactions.

To think about as you discuss . . .

- whether Haman saw this coming, or when he might have guessed it
- Xerxes' sudden realization that his top advisor threatened his queen

What does this mean to me?

- Reflect on a time when you had to make a difficult request. How did you handle your feelings? Were you doing this to stand up for what was right? How might Esther's example be helpful to you in the future?

Esther 7:7-10

3. How did Haman's reaction lead to a misunderstanding?

To think about as you discuss . . .

- why Xerxes left the banquet hall
- the tension in the air
- why Haman reacted the way he did

4. Discuss whether you think Haman got what he deserved.

To think about as you discuss . . .

- whether justice was served
- the irony that occurred in Haman's execution

What does this mean to me?

- Read **Lessons from History** (below) and discuss how we think about justice issues from a personal and a national point of view. Consider how the Bible can help us in thinking about these matters.

FLASHBACK

Some translations of the Bible say Haman was hanged, but it's more accurate to say he was impaled, as described in the TNIV.

Impalement was an act of torture and execution in which a person was pierced by a long stake. The stake would usually be planted in the ground, leaving the individual hanging to die.

The use of impalement as a form of execution in ancient Persia is evident in carvings from the ancient Middle East. According to Greek historian Herodotus (3.159), Darius I impaled 3,000 Babylonians when he took Babylon: this is recorded in the Behistun inscription.

Lessons from History

Haman stood in a long line of individuals who practiced genocide or wanted to. Even from recent history we can think of Adolf Hitler, Josef Stalin, Pol Pot, Saddam Hussein—the list goes on. The Bible offers insights into matters of personal justice and national justice.

- Romans 12:17-18 teaches us how to react on a personal level: "Do not repay anyone evil for evil. Be careful to do what is right in the eyes of everyone. If it is possible, as far as it depends on you, live at peace with everyone."
- In Romans 13:1-4 the apostle Paul teaches that we should respect the authorities who govern us. It's important to know that Paul wrote this at the time of the Roman Empire, in which a great deal of injustice occurred. Still, Paul wanted his readers to know they should do right as much as they could.
- We should not go against God's commands (for example, by bombing an abortion clinic or refusing to pay taxes), but we should resist a corrupt government if it is telling us to go against God's will. Christians during World War II hid Jews from the Nazis. Christians in Islamic countries today continue to tell people about Christ even though in some of those lands it is against the law (see Acts 4:18-20; 5:29). But it is God's place, not ours, to bring vengeance (Rom. 12:19). Despots and other tyrants may succeed for a while, but God will bring ultimate justice.

EPISODE 2

Esther 8:1-8

5. What did the king do for Esther and Mordecai?

To think about as you discuss . . .

- the vast wealth Haman had boasted about, and how this might benefit Esther, Mordecai, and their people
- why Esther might put Mordecai in charge of her property

6. Why did Esther risk an additional request?

To think about as you discuss . . .

- the urgency of this request, as well as Esther's risk in making it
- the king's response and how this would become law

Today we still sometimes use the expression **"like the law of the Medes and Persians,"** meaning that something could not be changed once it was decided (see Esther 1:7; 8:8; Daniel 6:8, 12, 15). Can you think of examples in which something like this happens today?

What does this mean to me?

- What does it feel like to "go to bat" (stand up) for someone, or to have someone do that for you?

Esther 8:9-14

7. How did the new edict provide protection for the Jewish people?

To think about as you discuss . . .

- what the new edict said, and how it would work against the edict Haman had written (see Esther 3:13). (*Note:* There'll be time to compare the two edicts in detail in the next lesson, so at this point you can focus mainly on the facts of the new edict in this setting.)
- the details of communicating and distributing the new edict

Imagine living in the far reaches of Xerxes' kingdom—around 1,200 miles (1,920 km) east or north or west of Susa (see map). Both the edict written by Haman and the one written by Mordecai could arrive at about the same time (the second edict went out on fast horses—see 8:10).

What would you make of these decrees?

Esther 8:15-17

8. Discuss the sudden turnarounds noted in these verses.

To think about as you discuss . . .

- how things changed for Mordecai and Esther and their people
- how the people of Jewish descent and other nationalities responded, and why they responded as they did

"Many people . . . became Jews" (Esther 8:17)—People sometimes change their religion to avoid being killed or simply to get along with others in the community around them. This is not genuine conversion, but it has often happened in history, especially in times of war. Some people change their religion after marrying into a family with a different religious background. We know that the Spirit of God is at work when people convert to belief in the one true God because they have developed a healthy fear of God, recognizing that the Lord is our Creator, Sustainer, and Savior from sin and death.

More to Think About

- Think about a time when you knew God was working behind the scenes in your life. What made you realize it was God? Did you recognize it at the time? Why or why not?

- If you are facing a difficult or frightening situation now (or if you may face one in the future), how can Esther's story help give you wisdom to handle that?

Famous preacher and seminary professor Haddon Robinson tells about being part of a gang when he was a young man. While on the way to a gang fight where he might have either killed someone or been killed, he tells how a police officer grabbed him and kicked him across the street. He has often stated that the foot of that policeman was the hand of God.

Explore!

- Learn about some other eucatastrophes in the Bible: Abraham and Isaac (Gen. 22:1-18), Moses and Israel at the Red Sea (Ex. 13:17-15:21), Naomi and Ruth (Ruth 1-4), Jonah and Nineveh (Jonah 1-4), Peter's escape from prison (Acts 12:1-17), and Paul and Silas and the Philippian jailer (Acts 16:16-34). Of course, the greatest eucatastrophe of all is Jesus' resurrection after dying for the sins of all who believe in him (see Luke 23-24; John 3:16).
- Check out biographies, documentaries, or movies on some of the following people (try googling them on the Internet): Corrie Ten Boom, Raoul Wallenberg, Dietrich Bonhoeffer, Alexander Solzhenitsyn, Rosa Parks, Martin Luther King, Jr. Compare their stories with that of Esther. What was similar? What was different?
- Draw a storyboard of a "coincidence" in your life that was really the hand of the invisible God working to help you.
- Consider some "do" responses to this lesson, perhaps like these:
  - Get into justice efforts such as support for the homeless, curbing the genocide in Darfur, or stopping unfair immigration practices.
  - Join a walk or another event to help fight poverty and hunger, or help out at a crisis pregnancy center.

Break Away (at-home readings)

Pride Before a Fall

God opposes the proud, but shows favor to the humble and
oppressed.   —1 Peter 5:5

The apostle Peter encourages us to clothe ourselves with humility (1 Pet.
5:5-6). We are to put on a humble spirit in much the same way we put on an
article of clothing. As we might choose an outfit or a suit for the morning,
we are to choose the way of humility rather than the way of pride.

Peter appears to have been thinking of Proverbs 3:34 when he reminds his
readers that those who choose humility receive God's grace. And, perhaps most important, he says that all the anxiety that comes when we are
mistreated can be cast on God (1 Pet. 5:7). God will help us and lift us up
because he cares for us. Our circumstances may not change immediately,
but our attitude can.

In what situations are you currently showing humility? Christ can give you
an appropriate humble spirit. When you begin to compare yourself to someone else, stop and compare yourself to Christ.   —DA

Ultimate Justice

The one in authority is God's servant for your good. But if you do
wrong, be afraid, for rulers do not bear the sword for no reason.
They are God's servants, agents of wrath to bring punishment on
the wrongdoer.   —Romans 13:4

Sometimes God uses those who govern us to bring about his justice. Even
though our earthly justice system is imperfect (and we should speak out
against it when it is), God can use people in authority to punish those who
do evil. In Romans 12:17 the apostle Paul says, "Do not repay evil for evil.
Be careful to do right in the eyes of everyone." Then in Romans 13:4 he

adds that the civil authorities can be agents of wrath to bring about God's punishment on those who do wrong.

Consider some situations or people you are dealing with. How would the knowledge that God ultimately deals justly improve your attitude and actions in those situations?   —DA

Revenge, Judgment

Seek the LORD, all you humble of the land, you who do what he commands. Seek righteousness, seek humility; perhaps you will be sheltered on the day of the LORD's anger.   —Zephaniah 2:3

Many people like to believe that God is a loving God who would not ever judge. But a God like that would not be truly loving or just. Zephaniah 2:1-3 reminds nations and people that God does not turn a blind eye to evil. Christians living in countries where there is extreme persecution, including torture, rape, and murder, find comfort in the fact that the Bible says God will judge evil someday. They know that even if their oppressors do not receive judgment in this lifetime, they will experience it in the end. This knowledge can help prevent these same Christians from being consumed with hatred and desire for revenge. As Romans 12:19 states, "Do not take revenge . . . but leave room for God's wrath, for it is written: 'It is mine to avenge; I will repay,' says the Lord" (see Deut. 32:35).

So, since God is both loving and just, how should this affect the way we live? Thank God for his gracious protection through Christ, who died in our place, so that we do not have to face God's anger. If we put our trust in Christ, we can be certain we will be sheltered from God's judgment. Pray that friends and family may understand the Lord's protection, and pray for Christians who are persecuted in our world today.   —DA

A Father and Son

God tested Abraham . . . [saying], "Take your son, your only son, whom you love—Isaac—and . . . sacrifice him . . . as a burnt offering. . . . Then [Abraham] reached out his hand and took the knife to slay his son. But the angel of the Lord called out to him from heaven. . . . "Do not lay a hand on the boy."   —Genesis 22:10-12

After looking at Genesis 22, we are hard pressed to find another story in the Old Testament that involves such a eucatastrophe (a sudden, happy turn of events). The nations around Abraham and his family sacrificed their children, but God never allowed this among his people.

How horrible that request must have been for Abraham! What amazing trust Abraham must have had in order to obey what God had said, particularly because Abraham had waited so many years for Isaac, the son of promise, to be born! What a happy turn of events it was when God provided a ram instead (Gen. 22:13). In the New Testament book of Hebrews we read that Abraham had so much trust in God that he knew God would raise Isaac from the dead if he had to (Heb. 11:17-19).

Let's thank God for all the great eucatastrophes in the Bible, especially the resurrection of his own Son, Jesus Christ, when all seemed lost after his death on the cross for our sake.

What near catastrophes—both great and small—in your life has God turned into eucatastrophes?   —DA

True Joy

The Lord has done great things for us, and we are filled with joy.
                                                      —Psalm 126:3

Psalm 126 describes the joy the people of Israel felt when they returned from exile to their homeland. This was the joy that comes when major circumstances in life change for the better.

In the book of Esther we read about some of the Jewish people who remained behind in the kingdom of Persia after many Jews had returned to Jerusalem and Judea. We don't know why they did not return to their homeland, but God still protected them. And when they experienced God's rescue from annihilation in Persia, as we read in the book of Esther, they too knew the meaning of great joy.

In 1 Peter 1:3-9 we have a description of even greater, "inexpressible and glorious" joy that gives happiness not only in this life but also in the life to come.

Try waking tomorrow morning and reflecting on something you can be joyful about. Remind yourself that because of Jesus we can be joyous in this life in spite of our circumstances. More important, we can know that if we place our faith and trust in Jesus, we can receive the salvation of our souls and everlasting life. —DA

Lesson 6
Victory and Celebration!

Esther 9-10

The empire is now preparing for the 13th day of the month of Adar. People are expecting that they may have to fight for their lives. The first edict (from Haman) is still in place, but another edict has also been written (by Mordecai) to allow the Jews to defend themselves.

Tension runs high. Anxiety fills the air. Danger looms with the threat of destruction. What will happen as the 13th arrives?

Opener (optional)

How do you react to a stressful situation?

A. __ Bite your nails.

B. __ Pace the room.

C. __ Eat whatever you can get your hands on.

Other _____

EPISODE 1

Esther 9:1-10

1. How do things go for the Jews on the 13th of Adar? For their enemies?

2. Describe the events in Susa. (See verses 6-10.)

To think about as you discuss . . .

- the time that has passed since the edicts were written (see Esther 3:12-13; 8:9-10), and how Mordecai's role has changed
- who is killed in Susa—and why

Comparing the Two Edicts

If we place the edicts of Haman and Mordecai side by side, we see similarities and one major difference. Though both were the king's edicts, they were written by very different people.

- **Haman's edict:** Esther 3:13-14—"Dispatches were sent by couriers to all the king's provinces with the order to destroy, kill and annihilate all the Jews—young and old, women and children—on a single day, the thirteenth day of the twelfth month, the month of Adar, and to plunder their goods."
- **Mordecai's edict:** Esther 8:11—"The king's edict granted the Jews in every city the right to assemble and protect themselves; to destroy, kill and annihilate the armed men of any nationality or province who might attack them and their women and children, and to plunder the property of their enemies."

If we looked only at the second edict, we might think the Jews were bloodthirsty and brutal. But to counter the first edict, the second one had to protect against the same evil commands written by Haman. The main difference in the second edict is in the words "protect themselves . . . to destroy . . . the armed men . . . who might attack them." In other words, the Jews had permission not to attack others but only to defend themselves.

The matter of plunder comes into perspective as well—the Jews *did not take any plunder* from those who attacked them, even though they had a right to. That fact is mentioned three times in Esther 9—in verses 10, 15, and 16.

What does this mean to me?

- How do you feel about the Jews' actions? Did they show recklessness or restraint? Explain.

- In what areas of our lives are we challenged to show self-control or restraint? How do we grow in self-control?

- Why is there sometimes so much hatred between different peoples?

- What are some examples of racism or other prejudice in our world today? What can we do about healing these problems?

Galatians 5:22-23 tells us, "The fruit of the Spirit is love, joy, peace, patience, kindness, goodness, faithfulness, gentleness and self-control. Against such things there is no law."

Esther 9:11-15

3. How does King Xerxes respond to the reports of the day?

To think about as you discuss . . .

- who the king asks for advice
- the threat that Haman's allies would have meant for the king

4. Why would Esther ask to extend the edict for one more day in Susa?

To think about as you discuss . . .

- that the Jews, a small minority among the powerful elite in Susa, had no right to attack but only to defend themselves (see "Comparing the Two Edicts" on the previous page)

5. What can we deduce from the fact that there was fighting in Susa on the next day, the 14th of Adar?

To think about as you discuss . . .

- what the Jews in Susa did, and what they refrained from doing
- additional comments in the "Q&A's" box on the next page

Notice that the Jews did not plunder their enemies' wealth, even though the edict allowed it (Esther 8:11). It's important to recognize the integrity of the Jews in the face of the temptation to seize the wealth of those who had taunted and oppressed them. Their self-restraint showed that their motive was self-defense.

Q&A's About Massacre Days

Q. Why would Xerxes have wanted Haman's friends and followers killed, apart from their threat to kill the Jews?

A. Haman had enjoyed great prestige in Susa. Any loyal followers would have been angered at his death and at the rise of Mordecai, and thus could have tried to overthrow the king. Considering the times in which this happened, it would commonly have been in the king's interest to destroy such enemies. The king also may have been angry that Haman had taken advantage of him—and thus wanted to make sure that others saw there were consequences for doing so.

Q. Was Esther asking for another day of bloodshed? Was she being cruel?

A. This question has perplexed a number of interpreters, but a straightforward explanation is possible, according to C. F. Keil and F. Delitzsch in their *Commentary on the Old Testament*. Note that the edict written by Mordecai gave Jews the right only to defend themselves against attackers. That right was granted only for the thirteenth day of Adar (to counteract the earlier edict written by Haman). Haman's edict, however, had called for annihilation of all the Jews (Esther 3:13). So, what if Haman's allies in Susa thought they should finish the job even if it weren't completed on the thirteenth day—that is, after the Jews' right to kill their attackers was removed? Even if making more attacks was illegal, that wouldn't stop powermongers in the political capital who might want to annihilate the Jews in Susa and then overthrow the king. As it turned out, another three hundred who hated the Jews did make attacks on them in Susa on the fourteenth day—and those enemies of the Jews were "put to death" (Esther 9:15). Keil and Delitzsch conclude that Esther's "foresight in securing the lives of her people against renewed attacks, betrays neither revenge nor cruelty" (p. 310).

Some of us might also wonder about the purpose of impaling (or hanging) ten men who were already dead (Esther 9:13). In those days such brutal actions often took place after a traitor was killed, as a way of displaying the body for public disgrace and as a warning to others.

Note also that we aren't told whether any Jews were killed in this horrible bloodbath. Historians say it wasn't common for victors to report losses among their own ranks. But we can surmise that some Jews probably were killed by people who attacked them—and yet the Jews "did not lay their hands on the plunder" of any of their enemies (Esther 9:10, 15-16).

Esther 9:16–19

6. Describe how things went differently in other parts of the empire. What were the results?

To think about as you discuss . . .

- what the Jews did on the 13th-15th days, and how they celebrated

EPISODE 2

Note: if you've been planning to share hamantaschen pastries during this lesson (see recipe at end of lesson 4), now would be a good time to enjoy them!

Esther 9:20-28

7. What does Mordecai urge the people to do?

To think about as you discuss . . .

- the purpose of celebrating
- how gift-giving would fit with celebrating God's goodness

8. Why is the celebration called Purim?

To think about as you discuss . . .

- the meaning of the name of this feast (see vv. 24, 26)
- how this celebration helps offer hope for the future

What does this mean to me?

- How do you celebrate what God has done in your life? Why is remembering God's acts of faithfulness important for us?

To Bless Others

The giving of gifts to the poor shows God's concern for all people. God had said to Abraham, ancestor of the Jews, "I will make you into a great nation, and I will bless you . . . and you will be a blessing. I will bless those who bless you, and whoever curses you I will curse; and all peoples on earth will be blessed through you" (Gen. 12:2-3).

Discuss how the story of Esther and Mordecai affirms God's promise of blessing and punishment. Note, too, that this means the Jews were spared not only for their own sake but also to bless others. Mordecai's command reveals an understanding of God's greater plan.

Reflect together on a question like this: *How can we be a blessing to others?*

Jewish dredel on the Hebrew script of Esther, traditionally read during celebration of Purim

Celebrating Purim!

Purim is one of the most joyous and fun holidays on the Jewish calendar. Celebration begins on the 14th day of Adar, which is usually in March. The word *Purim* means "lots" and refers to the lottery that Haman used to choose the date for the massacre (the 13th of Adar). The Purim holiday is preceded by a fast, the Fast of Esther, which commemorates Esther's three days of fasting in preparation for her meeting with the king.

The primary command related to Purim is to hear the reading of the book of Esther. This book is commonly known as the *Megillah*, which means "scroll." It is also customary to boo, hiss, stomp your feet, and rattle noisemakers whenever the name of Haman is mentioned during the reading. The purpose of this custom is to "blot out the name of Haman."

Participants also eat, drink, and celebrate. In addition, Jews are told to send out gifts of food or drink and to make gifts to charity. Among Ashkenazic (eastern European) Jews, a common treat at this time of year is hamantaschen ("Haman's pockets"; see Eat! at the end of lesson 4). It is also customary to hold carnival-like celebrations on Purim, to perform plays and parodies, and to hold beauty contests. Americans sometimes refer to Purim as the Jewish Mardi Gras.

—adapted from www.jewfaq.org/holiday9.htm. © 5756-5768 (1995-2008), Tracey R. Rich. Permission sought.

Esther 9:29-32

9. What is the purpose of Queen Esther's follow-up letter?

To think about as you discuss . . .

- how Esther's authority is now established
- how the people of the kingdom view Queen Esther

Traditional grogger (noise-maker) for celebrating Purim

What does this mean to me?

- What do you think of Esther? How has she grown?
  In what ways has her character remained the same?

- In what ways have you grown through this study of Esther?

The Dates of Purim

Notice the author's attention to the "designated" days of Purim (9:31; see 9:17-22). Jews throughout most of the empire feasted and celebrated on the 14th, but those in Susa were still fighting their enemies and delayed their feasting until the 15th. These two days became designated as the Feast of Purim, which came to be celebrated by rural Jews on the 14th and by urban Jews on the 15th.

Esther 10:1-3

10. What kind of leadership does Mordecai give to Xerxes' kingdom?

To think about as you discuss . . .
- how Mordecai's leadership and character compare to Haman's
- qualities that make a strong, effective leader

What does this mean to me?
- How has Jesus modeled leadership for us? (See Phil. 2:5-8.)

- Where has God placed you . . .
  —to serve?

  —to lead?

  —to rescue?

  —other?

> **For a couple of other examples** of wise, faithful believers who were blessed by God to become prominent leaders in a huge empire, see Genesis 41 and Daniel 6.

- How could you grow in service or leadership (or both), in God's strength, in the coming year?

Explore!

Try It Out

Esther and Mordecai instructed the Jews to continually celebrate this victory and this rescue from their enemies. How has God been at work in your family, your church, your community? Maybe you have experienced an amazing answer to prayer or God's continued faithfulness over the years. Create a celebration to remember something God has done. Decide on a date and a menu. Have fun. Don't forget to put it on next year's calendar too!

Taking It to Another Level

The story of Esther highlights a national conflict. There are similar kinds of conflicts happening all around the world today. As a group, choose a global or national conflict to learn more about. Gather information on who is involved and what has caused the conflict. Pray for the people involved, asking for peace and reconciliation in Jesus' name. Also look for ways to get involved—for example, with churches or medical or other helpful organizations in the conflict area.

Break Away (at-home readings)

Self-Control

The fruit of the Spirit is love, joy, peace, patience, kindness, goodness, faithfulness, gentleness and self-control. Against such things there is no law.   —Galatians 5:22

The Jews had been told they were going to be exterminated. According to the king's edict, neighbors could attack them and take all of their goods. Their children were under threat of death, and so were their friends and relatives. They were afraid, confused, and angry.

But then the tables turned. According to a second edict, the Jews could also defend themselves and plunder their enemies.

What would you do in their shoes? If given the upper hand, would you push to the limit? Take everything your enemies owned?

Surprisingly, the Jews left the plunder and limited the violence to the appointed days. What unnamed power enabled them to have such self-control? We know it was Yahweh, the God of the Bible, who gave us his Son, Jesus. We know today that Jesus challenged us to love our enemies and to pray for those who persecute us (Matt. 5:44). That's not easy! But Jesus himself showed unlimited self-control as his enemies persecuted him, accused him, and finally killed him. His self-control was an illustration of his love for us. Here is good news: Jesus gives us access to that same self-control through his Spirit.

In what situations do you need self-control? Is it about food, anger, unhealthy talk, or something else? Name it. Practice submitting your desires to God through the power of the Holy Spirit.   —SH

No Strings Attached

Do not repay anyone evil for evil. Be careful to do what is right in the eyes of everyone. If it is possible, as far as it depends on you, live at peace with everyone.   —Romans 12:17-18

The world is messy. It is marred by sin, hatred, and war. How do people who trust God deal with broken relationships and trouble? God gives us a surprising answer. Let God handle the punishment. He wants us to be in the business of loving others, seeking justice and feeding the hungry.

What would our world be like if we gave up our anger and showed love to others with no strings attached? Though we might not solve all the world's problems, we'd at least have immediate influence in our homes and relationships.

Is there anyone you have been hoping to punish? Will you let God handle that? Can you instead shower that person with love and peace?

In Romans 12:19-21 we read, "Do not take revenge, my dear friends, but leave room for God's wrath, for it is written: 'It is mine to avenge; I will repay,' says the Lord. On the contrary: 'If your enemy is hungry, feed him; if he is thirsty, give him something to drink. In doing this, you will heap burning coals on his head.' Do not be overcome by evil, but overcome evil with good."

—SH

Remember This

"Do this in remembrance . . ."   —Luke 22:19

Mordecai and Esther told the Jews to remember these days of victory and deliverance with a celebration. They were to call it *Purim,* the plural of the word *pur* (which means "lot"), to remember how Haman cast lots to determine which day to exterminate the Jews, and to remember how God miraculously worked behind the scenes to rescue them! Celebrate it this year and the next, they said to the people. Celebrate it with your descendants. Celebrate into the future because God is continually a God who rescues. Today Jews still follow Mordecai and Esther's advice by celebrating Purim.

Jesus has commanded us to celebrate God's rescue as well. Jesus was with his disciples the night before his death. On that night they celebrated the Passover dinner together, remembering God's great rescue of his people from slavery (see Ex. 12). From now on, Jesus said, as you celebrate this meal, remember that my death and resurrection provide the ultimate rescue (Luke 22:14-20). So today Christians everywhere remember Jesus' once-for-all rescue from sin by celebrating Holy Communion, or the Lord's Supper (also known as the Eucharist).

What can you do in memory of Christ today?   —SH

Humbled for Real Victory

Christ Jesus . . . humbled himself . . . . Therefore God exalted him to the highest place. . . . 　　　　　　　　　　　　　　—Philippians 2:5-9

Here is a picture of Jesus' life of humility followed by victory. Note that Jesus was willing to humble himself, trusting that God would exalt him at the proper time. Esther was called to do something similar when Mordecai said that she may have been chosen queen "for such a time as this" (Esther 4:14).

Where might you be called to humble yourself and let God do the exalting?

By the way, Jesus humbled himself all the way to the cross out of love for you and me and everyone else (Phil. 2:8). The forgiveness he earned is the forgiveness we all need.

Have you received his forgiveness along with his Holy Spirit and his promise of eternal life? If you haven't, try building a prayer out of these three words: *sorry, thank you, please.* (*For example:* I'm sorry for my sin. Thank you for your promise of forgiveness, the Holy Spirit, and eternal life. Please come into my life, forgive me, and help me to follow you.) 　　　　　　—SH

Getting the News Out

"You will be my witnesses . . . to the ends of the earth." 　　—Acts 1:8

In the book of Esther we've heard several times about spreading news throughout the Persian Empire—usually in the form of a decree. The last bit of news sent out had to do with the joyful celebration of Purim, and in this case "Mordecai sent letters to all the Jews in the 127 provinces" (Esther 9:30). This was good news that would affect all the people.

Nearly five centuries later Jesus came bringing the good news of God's kingdom and the offer of salvation for all people. Because of Jesus' life, death, and resurrection, we can now spread this good news everywhere.

So how are we getting the good news out today? It's happening through print, radio, TV, Internet, and other media; through preaching and teaching and Bible study in churches and schools and neighborhoods; through missionaries and aid workers and others who serve a worthy cause in Jesus' name. And in all these ways and more, it's happening (perhaps most effectively) by word of mouth.

When we become Jesus' witnesses, sharing God's love and good news with our neighbors and how it makes a difference in our lives, we're taking part in God's purpose for the world. We're helping to bring the good news "to the ends of the earth" (Acts 1:8) and to "be a blessing" to "all peoples" (Gen. 12:2-3). God worked through Esther and Mordecai to accomplish his purpose in their day; God can work through us today.

Take some time to think about ways you can be a witness to others about God's amazing works in your life. Don't worry that it may seem insignificant. Everything God does is important. Remember too that actions often speak louder than words. "Faith without deeds is dead" (James 2:26), and yet deeds without words can fall short of spreading the truth (about God) in love (see Eph. 4:15; 1 Pet. 3:15). Ask the Spirit to help you see ways in which you can share your story with others, and maybe help someone through a tough time or join in celebrating God's goodness together—or both!   —PF

The following invitation and prayer tools may be helpful to you in approaching God or in helping someone else do so.

An Invitation

Listen now to what God is saying to you. Maybe you are aware of things in your life that keep you from coming near to God. Maybe you have thought of God as someone who is unsympathetic, angry, and punishing. You may feel as if you don't know how to pray or how to come near to God.

"But because of his great love for us, God, who is rich in mercy, made us alive with Christ even when we were dead in transgressions—it is by grace you have been saved" (Eph. 2:4-5). Jesus, God's Son, died on the cross to save us from our sins. It doesn't matter where you come from, what you've done in the past, or what your heritage is. God has been watching over you and caring for you, drawing you closer. "You also were included in Christ when you heard the word of truth, the gospel of your salvation" (Eph. 1:13). Do you want to follow Jesus? It's as simple as A-B-C:

- **A**dmit that you have sinned and you need God's forgiveness.
- **B**elieve that God loves you and that Jesus has already paid the price for your sins.
- **C**ommit your life to God, asking the Lord to forgive your sins, nurture you as his child, and fill you with the Holy Spirit.

Prayer of Commitment

Here is a prayer of commitment recognizing Jesus as Savior. If you want to be in a loving relationship with Jesus Christ, pray this prayer. If you have already committed your life to Jesus, use this prayer for renewal and praise.

Dear God, I'm sorry for the wrong and sinful things that I've done. I need your forgiveness. I know I need Jesus as my Savior, and I know you listen to sinners who are truthful to you. Please forgive me and help me to live in a right relationship with you.

Thank you, Jesus, for dying on the cross to pay the price for my sins. Father, please take away the guilt that I feel because of my sin, and bring me into your presence. Thank you, Lord, for loving me and saving me.

Holy Spirit of God, help me to pray, and teach me to live by your Word. Help me to follow you faithfully. Make me more like Jesus each day, and help me to share your love and good news with others everywhere. In Jesus' name, Amen.

Bibliography

Alexander, David and Pat, et al., eds. *Eerdmans' Handbook to the Bible.* Grand Rapids, Mich.: Wm. B. Eerdmans, 1992.

Barker, Kenneth L., and John R. Kohlenberger III. *Zondervan NIV Bible Commentary.* Grand Rapids, Mich.: Zondervan, 1994.

Boomsma, Sylvia, and Edith Bajema. *Discover Esther* (Leader Guide). Grand Rapids, Mich.: Faith Alive Christian Resources, 1991, 2003.

Elwell, Walter A., ed. *Baker Encyclopedia of the Bible.* Grand Rapids, Mich.: Baker Book House, 1988.

Guthrie, D., and J. A. Motyer, et al., eds. *The New Bible Commentary: Revised.* Grand Rapids, Mich.: Wm. B. Eerdmans, 1970.

Inspirit Bible study series. Grand Rapids, Mich.: Faith Alive Christian Resources, 1995.

Keil, C. F., and F. Delitzsch. *Commentary on the Old Testament.* Grand Rapids, Mich.: Wm. B. Eerdmans, 1975.

New Interpreter's Bible, The. Vol. 3. Nashville: Abingdon Press, 1999.

Peterson, Eugene. *Eat this Book.* Grand Rapids, Mich.: Eerdmans, 2006.

TNIV Study Bible. Grand Rapids, Mich.: Zondervan, 2006.

Evaluation Questionnaire

INFUSE - Esther: Courage in a Complicated World

As you complete this study, please fill out this questionnaire to help us evaluate the effectiveness of our materials. Please be candid. Thank you.

1. Was this a home group _____ or a church-based _____ program?
   What church?

2. Was the study used for
   _____ a community evangelism group?
   _____ a community faith-nurture group?
   _____ a church Bible study group?

3. How would you rate the materials?
   Study Guide   _____ excellent _____ very good _____ good_____ fair_____ poor
   Leader's Notes on website   _____ excellent _____ very good _____ good_____ fair_____ poor

4. What were the strengths?

5. What were the weaknesses?

6. What would you suggest to improve the material?

7. In general, what was the experience of your group?

Your name (optional) _____

Address _____

_____

8. Other comments:

(Please fold, tape, stamp, and mail. Thank you.)

Faith Alive Christian Resources
2850 Kalamazoo Ave. SE
Grand Rapids, MI 49560